Usborne

Wipe-Clean Dot-to-Dot

Farm

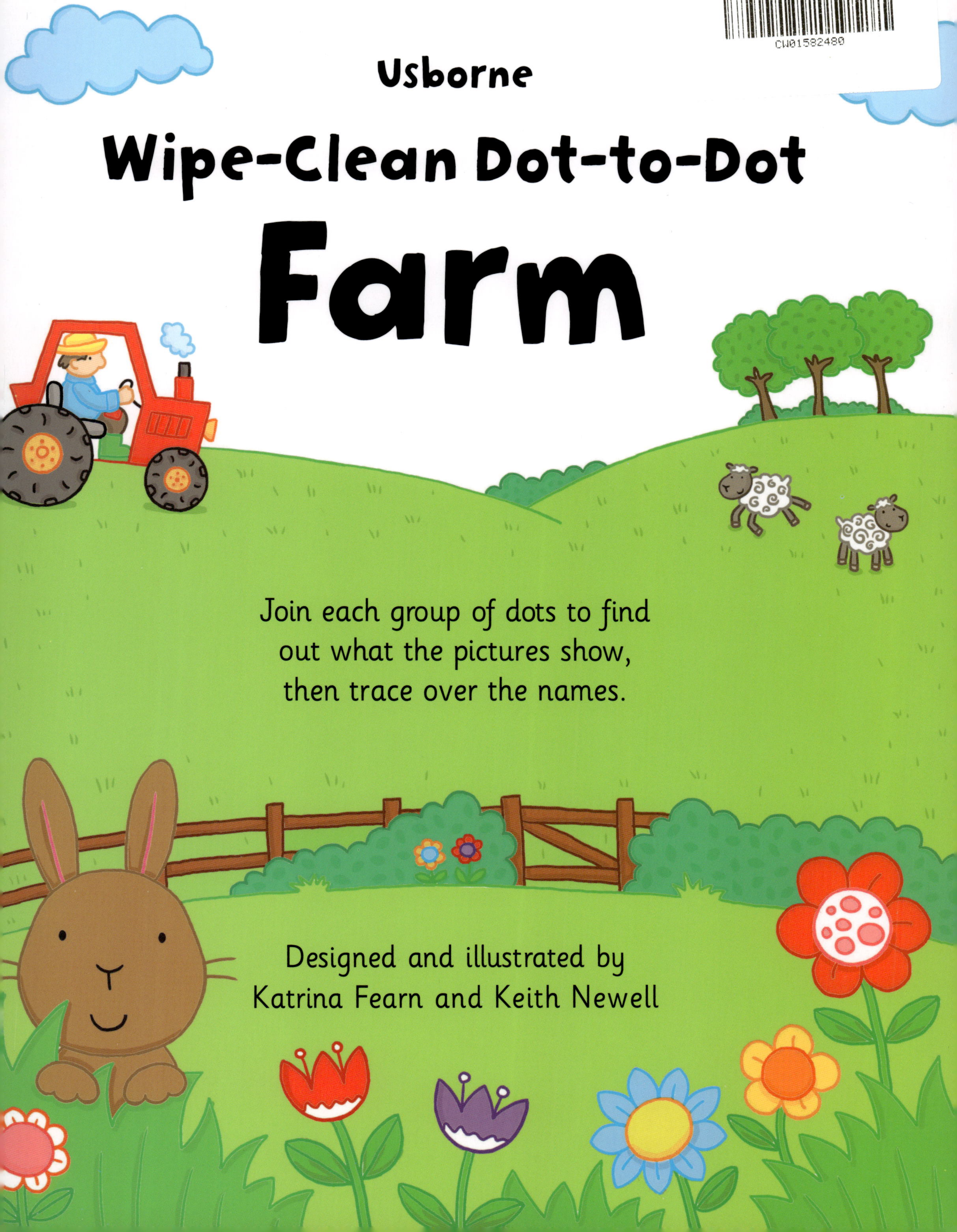

Join each group of dots to find out what the pictures show, then trace over the names.

Designed and illustrated by
Katrina Fearn and Keith Newell

1 2 3 4 5 6 7 8 9 10

Who has two horns and a little beard?

a b c d e f g h i j k l m

Who is looking after her chicks?

hen

1 2 3 4 5 6 7 8 9 10

Who says 'moo'?

COW

Who likes to run in the field?

a b c d e f g h i j k l m n o p q r s t u v w x y z

1 2 3 4 5 6 7 8 9 10

Who likes to eat carrots?

a b c d e f g h i j k l m

Where does the hen live?

henhouse

1 2 3 4 5 6 7 8 9 10

What is the farmer driving?

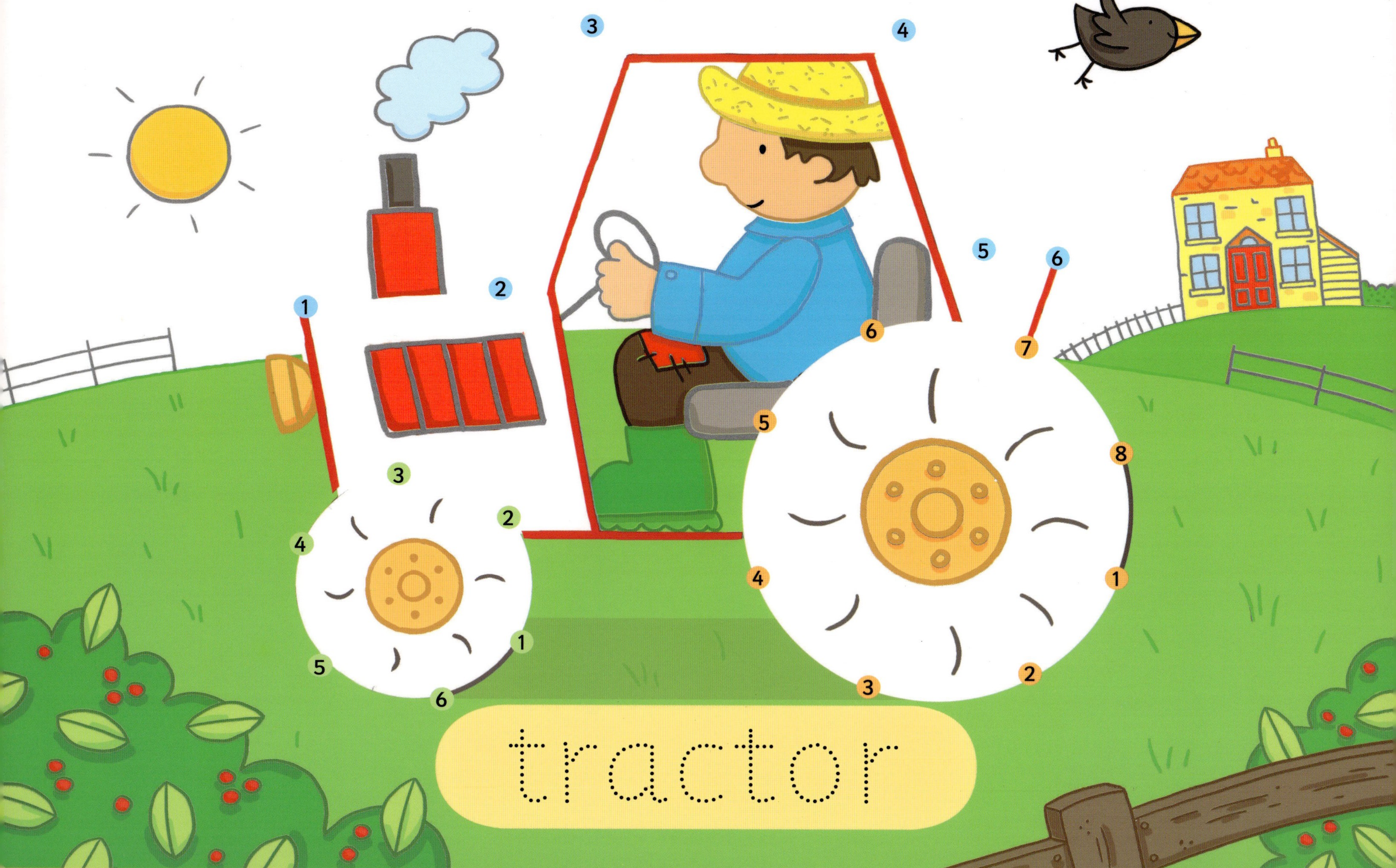

Who says 'baa'?

sheep

a b c d e f g h i j k l m n o p q r s t u v w x y z

1 2 3 4 5 6 7 8 9 10

Who is standing in the field?

a b c d e f g h i j k l m

Who has big orange feet?

1 2 3 4 5 6 7 8 9 10

Who is paddling in the pond?

Where does the farmer live?

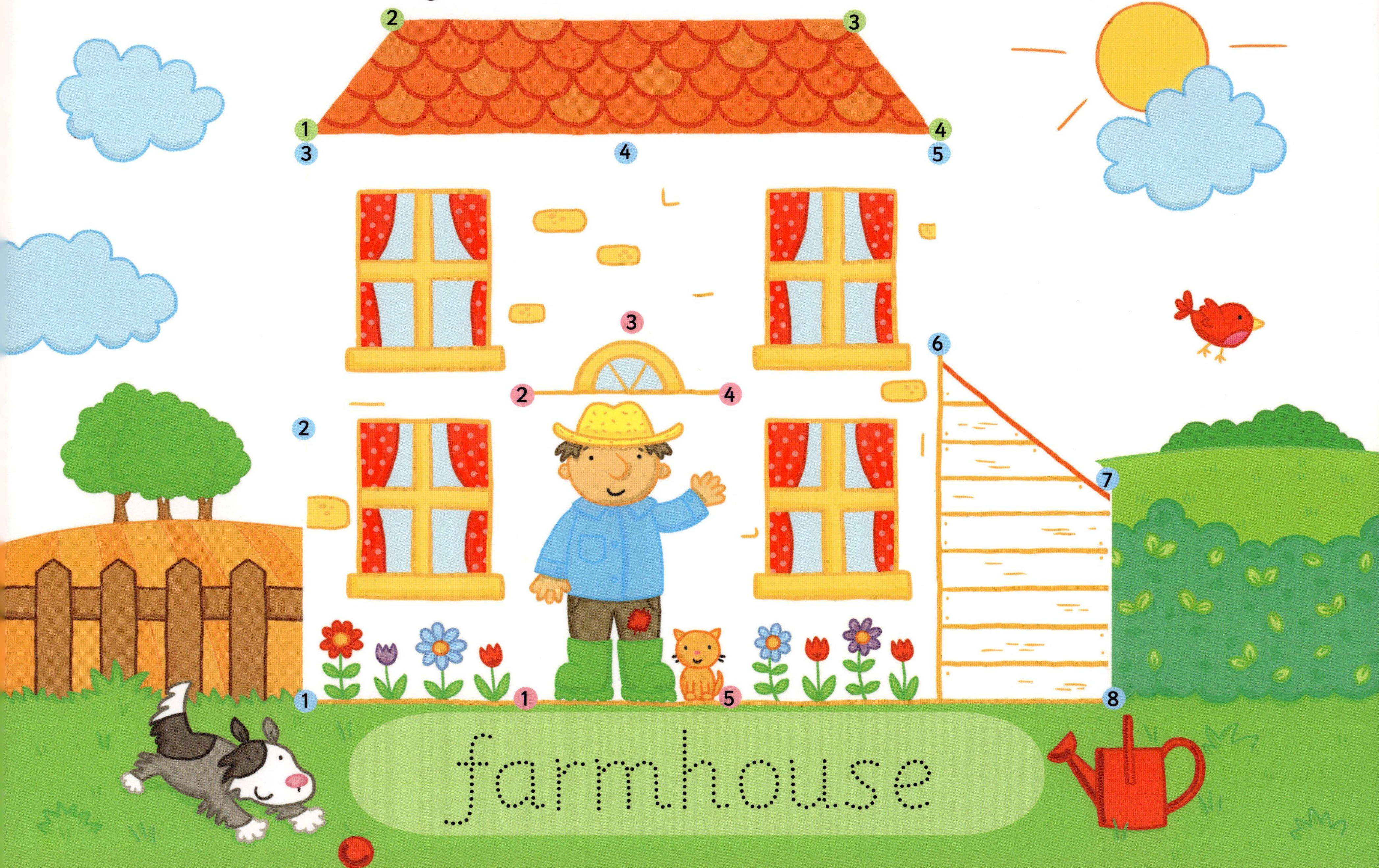

a b c d e f g h i j k l m n o p q r s t u v w x y z

Who has a long tail and four hooves?

horse

1 2 3 4 5 6 7 8 9 10

Who is wearing muddy boots?

n o p q r s t u v w x y z

1 2 3 4 5 6 7 8 9 10

Where does the tractor live?

Who moves very, very slowly?

a b c d e f g h i j k l m n o p q r s t u v w x y z

Usborne

Wipe-Clean Dot-to-Dot

Farm

Joining dots and tracing over letters are fun ways for children to practise counting, writing and pen control.

www.usborne.com

£5.99
CAD $10.95

JFMAMJJASO D/18
03549/06

CE

WARNING! Not suitable for children under 36 months because of small parts. Choking hazard.

ATTENTION! Ne convient pas aux enfants de moins de 36 mois en raison des petites pièces. Risque de suffocation par ingestion.

Ink from pen may not be washable.
L'encre du feutre ne s'efface pas toujours au lavage.

Made with paper from a sustainable source.

ISBN 978-1-4095-8753-8
9 781409 587538 >

First published in 2015 by Usborne Publishing Ltd., Usborne House, 83–85 Saffron Hill, London EC1N 8RT, England.

UKE. Printed in Shenzhen, Guangdong, China.

1 2 3 4 5 6 7 8 9 10